COUNTY O

COUNTY O

POEMS BY ROBERT HEDIN

Copper Canyon Press

Grateful acknowledgment is made to the following periodicals and anthologies in which many of these poems appeared:

Beloit Poetry Journal, Chowder Review, Copperhead, Dacotah Territory, Epoch, Free Passage, Great Circumpolar Bear Cult, Great River Review, Greenfield Review, Iron (UK), *Kansas Quarterly, Permafrost, Poetry, Poetry Now, Poetry Review* (UK), *Porch, Portland Review, Puerto Del Sol, Southern Poetry Review, Sou'wester, The Ark, Three Rivers Poetry Journal, Twelve Poems, Willow Springs Magazine.*

Anthology of Magazine Verse and Yearbook of American Poetry (Monitor Book Co., Inc.), *Dacotah Territory* (North Dakota Institute of Regional Studies), *Rain in the Forest, Light in the Trees: Contemporary Poetry from the Northwest* (Owl Creek Press).

"On Tuesdays They Open The Local Pool To The Stroke-Victims" and "Tornado" ("Four farms over it looked like a braid of black hemp . . .") were originally published in *Poetry*.

Several of these poems also appeared in slightly different versions in *Snow Country* and *At the Home-Altar* (Copper Canyon Press), and *On the Day of Bulls* (Jawbone Press Pamphlet Series).

Publication of this book is made possible in part by a grant from the National Endowment for the Arts, a federal agency. Copper Canyon Press is in residence at Centrum.

Copper Canyon Press, Box 271, Port Townsend, WA 98368

FOR CAROLYN

Contents

I

The Snow Country

—*for Carolyn*

Up on Verstovia the snow country is silent tonight.
I can see it from our window,
A white sea whose tide flattens over the darkness.
This is where the animals must go—
The old foxes, the bears too slow to catch
The fall run of salmon, even the salmon themselves—
All brought together in the snow country of Verstovia.
This must be where the ravens turn to geese,
The weasels to wolves, where the rabbits turn to owls.
I wonder if birds even nest on that floating sea,
What hunters have forgotten their trails and sunk out of sight.
I wonder if the snow country is green underneath,
If there are forests and paths
And cabins with wood-burning stoves.
Or does it move down silently gyrating forever,
Glistening with the bones of animals and trappers,
Eggs that are cold and turning to stones.
I wonder if I should turn, tap and even wake you.

Herds

On clear nights when I walk
The path back home,
I see animals glistening with frost
High in the grasslands.

Legends say they are small
Seas of breath
Stranded from an age lit by snow,
That when thaw comes

They stray through the foothills,
Leaving a strange language
Free in the streams,
Herds of lichen grazing on stones.

Goddard Hot Springs

When you lie in these sweating streams
You are lying in the breath of your ancestors,
The old pioneers who sat here in these pools
Mapping trails to the mother lode.
You feel a fog drift through your body,
A voice that is strangely familiar
And still has stories to tell.

Ancestors

—for Robert Davis

The Indians on this island tell a story about fog.
They say in its belly
The spirits of the drowned are turned into otters
That on cold nights when the lowlands
Smolder with steam
The loon builds its nest in their voices.
And I remember you telling me
Of a clan of friends you had heard in a dream
All quietly singing to themselves.
Ancestors you said
People you hadn't seen in years
Each wrapped in otter
And offering a piece of last month's moon—
A small amulet that glittered in the dark like bone.
And all around you could see baskets of berries
Glistening with rain
And deep in the fog fish sweetening on the racks.

Pilot, Drowned Young

When the night-fishermen spotted you
In the light off the jetty,
You were balled-up and bloomed,
Shimmering like a jewel.
And somehow the sea believed,
And took you in.
For days, my friend,
The fishermen talked of your spine.
They said it glistened in the dark like coral.
Ted, I imagine you camped
Where that old salmon-wheel smolders
In the moonlight.
Friend of the loons,
You wear their pearls like amulets.
And I dream you are building a cockpit
Out of kelp and seaweed,
That you drift naked in the rain—
A pilot for all the salmon that come
To drown in the air.
You sing, and plunge, and bank
Into the dead calm.
And somehow the sea believes.

Kelp-Cutters

Ten years since I buried
All the air I could,
And followed you
Down into that cold,
Seeing your breath shimmer
Like stars on the kelp.
Joe, when we broke through
That last time and found
The boat gone, the air
So cold we lay there
Not saying a word,
Hand in hand, treading
Until your warm grip went slack—
Joe, I could do nothing
But ride with the kelp
Into dawn, rocking
In the cold slate,
Listening to myself pump
The damp night full of breath.

Sitka Spruce

I swear these trees come from before,
Dumb stragglers from the edge.
In their trunks the fossil worm still sings.
In the shade of each branch
There are crickets still barking like sea lions.
Legends tell of main veins shooting
Deep into the earth
To feed off pools of red lava,
That some run south along the fault lines,
Churning through coastal bays and inlets—
And when a Latin peasant clears his land
The cutting and crackling of roots
Is felt here, far north
Where a tree will shiver and shed one cone.

2.

My wife and I watch the orphan trunks
Ride with the tides back to the land.
They roll and slide like whales,
Their smooth brown backs flashing in the sun.
We have seen them drifting in the Bering,
Following the songs of seals—
Uncut totems beautifully round and faceless,
Waiting for the masks of ancient clans
To rise, and chant again like the winds
That draw the foam from the sea.

3.

I have heard that when we die
These spruce will take and mother the moon.
We will find it nestled among the roots,
In a crowd of friends,
A child with a quarter face.
Stepping forward it will offer us
A gift wrapped in moss—
A pale cone out of which we pick the sharpest teeth,
And opening our hands we prick our palms,
And watch as the first seeds of blood
Trickle and combine into pools,
Rich seas the roots curl and slide for.

Owls

—for William Pitt Root

Owls glide off the thin
Wrists of the night,
And using snow for their feathers
Drift down on either side
Of the wind.

I spot them
As I camp along the ridge,
Glistening over the streambeds
Their eyes small rooms
Lit by stone lamps.

Last Poet

This man is a lover
Of canyon walls.
The first to read by moon alone.

During the day
He lives away from the sun,
Prone in the cool dirt
Under ledges,
Revising that one long last narrative line
On sheets of mica.

Now is the time
He chooses his closest friends:
A piece of jagged rock,
A cricket who's run out of songs.

Near evening
He makes his way to a precipice
And scours
The stones for scratches
Other than his own.

And as the moon curls over the rim
He recites his work
From memory,
Then listens as the canyon reads back
Again and again.
And then he claps
And the whole canyon applauds.

Transcanadian

At this speed our origins are groundless.
We are nearing the eve of a great festival,
The festival of wind.
Already you can see this road weakening.
Soon it will breathe
And lift away to dry its feathers in the air.
On both sides the fields of rapeseed and sunflowers
Are revolting against their rows.
Soon they will scatter wildly like pheasants.
Now is the time, my friend, to test our souls.
We must let them forage for themselves,
But first—unbuckle your skin.
Out here, in the darkness
Between two shimmering cities,
We have, perhaps for the last time, chance
Neither to be shut nor open, but to let
Our souls speak and carry our bodies like capes.

End

At the end of the open road we come to ourselves
—Louis Simpson

All right, Louis
        we're here
We're here at the end of the open road,
At the end of our ellipsis.

A wind and slight drizzle hide
Any other footprints.
They curl the road
Around our feet,
Sweeping it back into itself.

Louis, in the darkness we think
We see trees, giant sequoias
That break around an open marsh,
And are compelled to give them green,
To give them sway,
A hard mossy bark,
Rain dripping from their leaves.

Listen. A bullfrog's call.
Smell the wet calm in the air.

We wait for the moon,
For the song of a white bird

Any backdrop
        of light.

II

At Betharram

Here a mile down at Betharram
The grottos start winding
Through the earth.
The walls seep
With last year's rain,
And I go down, alone, breathing
An air that's never
Been breathed.
And the farther I go
The more I want it like this in the end—
The earth empty,
My lantern going out in the cold,
The stalactites burning
Like huge wet roots
In the dark.
There's a calm here at Betharram
Deeper than I have known.
And down this far,
The heart slows and beats
As calmly as the water
That never stops,
That I hear
Far down in the caves,
Dripping for miles through stone.

Sainte-Foy

In the Pyrenees they killed
Their animals with stones,
And before that by running
Their herds into the blazing
Air off these foothills.
Here at the church of Sainte-Foy,
The blood of those animals
Comes back night after night.
It comes back as dust
On the old stone cutter,
The Bernais I see walking
At sundown up the long
Rocky path. It comes back
As earth and stone, as hard
Chunks of mortar and clay
I pull from the wall
And smell what is Sainte-Foy.
There's a silence so deep
I could stay here and breathe
This cold forever,
All this dung and hay,
This wet uncut stone—
A vow I take deep, and break
As my headlights go on,
And see in the graveyard out back,
Snout buried in mud and clay,
A hog big enough for slaughter,
A loose sow that grunts once
At my lights, and doesn't move.
She stands there as I turn,

And the night comes on—
Her ears and round pink back
Steaming in the cold—
Feeding on the dead,
And what the dead push up.

December 31, 1977

And my boy beside me sick
At the new year,
Sick in this place
He could never call home.
And all I can do is reach out and feel
For his chest, feel and come
To something warm and bare,
A grave no larger
Than my hand.
Alexander, if the year turns,
It will leave nothing
But a light too weak
To bless, nothing
But the water
I drew from the earth
At dusk, a cupful
As cold and still as any
I ever brought to your lips.
You, a small armful of bones
Your mother breathed
Into the gray mist
At dawn, held
Here as nothing
I haven't held before—
A cough, a fever that won't break,
A heart that rises and falls
Under my palms—
A flower
Breathing all it was given,
All it was left, and nothing more.

A year dead and gone,
Another in my arms
Starting up
Deep in your lungs as blood.

The Shrine of Tanit

Carthage

First the Romans and then the Vandals
Came here to burn and gut this old city.
And now us, and that little Arab boy
Hunting for Phoenician lamps
And old Roman coins along the dry hillsides.
It's June, and late in the day,
And my son stands beside me,
My first and only son who is three
And doesn't understand why we've come
To stare out at this huge field of mustard.
I want to tell him the earth here
Is warmer than any house he has known,
And that beneath us now are bones
No bigger than his fingers,
Row upon row of first-born buried
Under these burning slabs of stone,
All ground down to the age of the earth.
We stand here as the dusk comes on,
Both of us waiting for his mother
To walk in out of this field.
The mustard she's picked
Will be brought back, dried and pressed,
And arranged until each bright tip
Burns like a star,
And is martyred each time
This field blooms, or darkens into seed.

The Northern Edge at Douz

Here on the northern edge
Of these great sand
And salt flats,
Half the night is gone
And those of us gathered
In the heat and
Dead calm at Douz
Are waiting for the one
Bus to take us out
The way we came—
The young Garde Nationale
Who for three days
Has stared at the sand
In his beer, the old man
Who was here for Rommel
And who'll be here
When little Said drives
His goats up the dry riverbed,
Bringing word from the sand
And Four Winds, from all
The heat and sweat,
The salt that is boiled
And rinsed, that will burn
Like tears down
The length of his face.
Here in Douz, the only
Star up is the one
Bulb hanging by its wires
In the empty doorway,
Casting light on the black
Lamb that was drained

At dusk in the schoolyard,
Its veins and warm smooth
Throat slit for all of us
Who've waited this night out,
And are too tired
To talk the long dawn
Out of coming on, to stop
The lamb from bleeding, unable
To catch the blood
Before it cools
And is mistaken for rain.

On the Day of Bulls

4:30 a.m., the room quiet,
And I have made it
Longer through the night
Than the streetlight
That flickered
And died
In the courtyard.
In another hour it'll be dawn,
And already too late
To ask anything
Of the day,
Of this rain beating
Against the flat
Slate roofs
Of this city.
Nine floors below
On the Boulevard Ornano,
The fruit and vegetable stalls
Stand beside the small
Iron scales tipped
All night by the rain,
The burning leaves
Of the eucalyptus
Are waiting
To strike
The earth and go out.
I think of the bullet
You write about,
And how it lies there
Snug as a seed
Against your spine;

Of the police in Pamplona
Who'll wake on this day
To find the rain
Beating down
Out of a black sky,
Rain that's fallen all night
To cool the sores
Of the dying,
Rain that'll never once
Let the dead forget
What it's like
To live on this earth;
And of all the bulls
Kept lean on the bare hillsides,
The bulls that will die
All over Spain
Without ears.
And finally of you
Having to live out this night
Blessed by your own sweat,
Unable to flex
Your toes,
Or feel the muscles
That went soft as a child's.
Only now in the last hour
Before sunrise
Can you love
This earth,
Its deep stillness,
And the way another day
Comes on without pain.

        —for Philippe,
            shot in the Basque riots,
            Pamplona, 1978

At the Olive Grove of the Resistance

He says that home is here,
Here where the earth falls apart
In our hands, and he points
To the one good eye they left him;
Half his world cut out, half
Buried here in the charred roots
Of his three olive trees, four fingers
Down where they made him go
On his knees, his face sliced
To the bone; left him here
To look up and see his oxen
Riding a crown of blood
Into the hills, his trees
Burning, each small olive
Blazing into light; left him
To stumble back up the hill
To find his son face-down
On the stone pathway, his wife
In the shed sprawled on the bags
Of seed, her white breasts
Bruised; left him to wander
Each night in the wind
Born in these black branches,
Or to stand in his small stone room
Spreading the olives out
Like jewels in the sink. And
He tells me the good ones
Go north so he can pay
For the luxury of this light,
The one bare bulb that's the only
Flower of his house. And

Because I am new and have come
Here to listen, he cuts one open
And shows me its hard oily pit,
A small black stone that lies here
In his palm, drying in the wind
Brought out of his three olive trees.

The Bombing of Dresden

It was the night of Fasching,
And those crossing
The Marienbrucke
Saw the cold drizzle,
And the black winter sky
Suddenly ignite into summer;
Saw the sap come back
And burn like sweat
On the skins
Of trees. And for an hour
The pipes in every cellar
Dripped and ran dry,
The glass doorknobs flowered
Into jewels,
And the grapes
That were left out
To smolder on their vines
Swelled and burst
Into stones. And for an hour
The earth was a jar,
And every beet
And potato inside
Thawed and began to bleed.
The next morning those gathered
Along the Elbe saw the cold
Smoke of a blossom,
And couldn't be sure
It was dawn,
That what they saw
Was the sun striking a fish
And the singed weaving

Of its gills.
And nothing
Was left of the cows,
Or the fields that had come back
To burn like goldenrod,
Nothing but the snails
Gripping the dry
Walls of the cisterns,
The snails that overnight
Turned into limestone to survive.

Waiting For Trains At Col d'Aubisque

4 a.m. and rain since dark, rain dropping
From the slate roofs onto the stone walkway,
And all of us here—
The middle-aged mother and the child,
The three privates smoking
As only those going off
For good can smoke—
All of us standing at these windows,
Except the young boy out under the archway
Who has brought his father's coffin
Down out of these bare hills,
A small sheepherder's boy
Who doesn't care how old the night gets
Or how long this rain takes hold,
Only that his wool coat
Is folded neatly, and that his head rests
Over his father's shoulder,
For if this boy, this young dark-eyed Basque
From Col d'Aubisque
Whose skin will never again feel as wet
Or as wanted as it is
By all this rain,
If this small boy would talk
He would say we've stood all night
At these windows for nothing,
And that even if the morning comes
And we step out into the cold light,
Finding the world no better or worse
And ourselves still wanting
To be filled with its presence,

The words we've waited all night to say
We will have to turn into breath
And use to warm our hands.

III

Eclipse

Father
I have come back
To this squat Minnesota town

This shrinking house
These bald fall rooms
To find you in a stack

Of dim photos
Curled like leaves
In the back of a drawer

I run my thumb
Over your face
And feel the glassy

Bristles of your mustache
The creases
Along your cheeks

We stare at each other
And I feel you
Lose your gloss

You draw me downward
Page by page
Photo by photo

Until your body is warm
And massive and my hand
Loses itself in yours

We stand on Sorin's Bluff
And watch the wind
Die in the elms

Our shadows melt
Into one another
As we squint

Through two worn negatives
At the moon sliding
Across the sun

The valley darkens
And I am left blind
Until the sun jumps

And catches the trees
Until the moon
And you Father fade

And leave me
Holding these cold
Exposures

This reverse bond
From which I pull myself
Head-first

To grip the first
Warm object
I see

The Wreck of the Great Northern

Where the Great Northern plunged in
The river boiled with light, and we all stood
In the tall grass staring at a tangle
Of track, and four orange coaches
And one Pullman lying under the current,
Turning the current clear. We stood staring
As though it had been there all along
And was suddenly thrust up out of the weeds
That night as a blessing, as a long sleek hallway
Dropping off into fields we'd never seen,
Into the pastures of some great god
Who sent back our steers too heavy to move,
All bloated and with green seaweed strung down
Their horns. And we all looked down
Into the lit cars at businessmen
And wives, already back to breathing water,
And saw in the cold clear tanks of the Pullman
A small child the size of my son, a porter's
White jacket, a nylon floating gracefully
As an eel.
              What the train and the river
Were saying, no one could understand.
We just stood there, breathing what was left
Of the night. How still the cars were,
How sleek, shimmering through the undertow.
And I saw the trees around us blossomed out,
The wind had come back and was blowing
Through the tall empty grass, through the high
Grain fields, the wind was rattling
The dry husks of corn.

Rattlesnake Bluff

That night the lack of rain brought them
Down off the bluff,
All we saw was the grass
Fluttering where we'd burned,
And occasionally in the hot flashes
Of light, a long body stretched out off the porch
Shimmering in the dew. The next morning
When we found the hens dead
In the yard, the froth
On the cow's udder,
The skin wrapped like jewelry
Around the cold jars of preserves,
You loaded the gun and we climbed half-way up
The huge slope, leading each other around
Until we found one
As thick as our wrists,
So sluggish it could only dive once
And miss. When you pulled
And its head flew off like a bottlecap,
What little water the earth had given up
Was only good for cooling
Our hands, for wiping
The long blade after the rattles were loose.

Sloughing

Back here in the bottomlands
The sloughs lie flat
As hides, breathing quietly
Among dead trees
And reeds. It is June,
Almost fifteen years
Since we stripped
And waded into those warm
Lungs, drifting among turtles
And sunfish, in what was dying
Or dead, or having to grow
Simple to survive.
You stood there knee-deep
In the smoke off the water,
Naked and wet with algae,
The old rotted shell
You'd found lifted up
Into the cold light
Like a horn, a white strand
Of fish-eggs strung down
Dripping from your neck like seeds.

Tornado

On Saturdays we chose Lyle
Catcher for both sides.
He was one of the slow ones,
And was around only
To lob the balls back,
Or to chase our long flies
Into the graveyard
Behind Our Lady of the Fields.
The night it came sweeping down,
Long, dark, a root dropping
As low as any crop duster,
We were under the pews,
Everyone but Lyle,
And could tell it touched close
By the way the long
Bell rope danced.
We were only nine,
And hid there
Until the calm came back,
Until everything started to steam—
The fields, the gravestones,
The cracked troughs
Of holy water—
Even the fish Lyle was parading
Around the infield,
The fat gray carp he said
Had come swimming down
Out of the clouds.
Perhaps it was the way
He was breathing,
Or how he held it up

To show the blood on its gills
That made us all believe
He had caught it over home plate,
Right where he had lost
So many in the sun.

Houdini

There is a river under this poem.
It flows blue and icy
And carries these lines down the page.
Somewhere beneath its surface
Lying chained to the silt
Harry holds his breath
And slowly files
His fingernails into moons.
He wonders who still waits at the dock
If the breasts of those young girls
Have developed since he sank.
He thinks of his parents
Of listening to the tumblers
Of his mother's womb
Of escaping upward out of puberty
Out of the pupils in his father's eyes
And those hot Wisconsin fields.
He dreams of escaping from this poem
Of cracking the combinations
To his own body
And those warm young safes
Of every girl on the dock.
Jiggling his chains
Harry scares a carp that circles
And nibbles at his feet.
He feels the blue rush of the current
Sweeping across his body
Stripping his chains of their rust
Until each link softens
And glows like a tiny eel.
And Harry decides to ascend.

He slips with the water through his chains
And moving upward
Climbing over and over his own air bubbles
He waves to the fish
To his chains glittering
And squirming in the silt.
He pauses to pick a bouquet
Of seaweed for the young girls on the dock.
Rising he bursts the surface of this poem.
He listens for shouts.
He hears only the night
And a buoy sloshing in the blue.

Gravediggers

They have done this so long
They could do it blind,
And some have—
This stocking every year
Of the dead's pond,
This going around at night
Closing all the flowers.
Yesterday I was sure
I could hear the screams
In the backs of their throats,
My neighbor's cats pacing
Down there in little
Cages of bone.
They are blameless
But that doesn't stop them
From digging, from winding
Their gold watches,
From staring out
Of their sheds when it's hot,
When all they can hear
Is the click-click
Of the sprinklers,
Like so many locks coming undone.

Hunting Agates At White Rock

All day alone and stripped to the waist,
The sweat gleaming on the hairs
Of my stomach. Two miles
South in the gravel pit
At White Rock, and there's nothing
But my own breath going out
Among these stones. Where is the tooth
My grandfather unearthed here,
The mastodon molar as big and brown
As his old gnarled fist? Or the rock
I heaved at the harmless bullsnake,
And the light burning that day
Off the stones? As a child
I remember going silent for days,
Trying to hear how the earth sounds
To the dead, and hearing
The huge silver tumbler in the cellar
Grinding the stones day and night,
Until they came out gray
With sludge and needed washing
Under the hose. Now there is nothing
But the earth at White Rock
Lying open like a grave,
With just enough light to gather
My stones. Soon the winds will come,
And the first martins flying
For the night into the bottomlands,
The heat lightning a mile out
Over the flood plains. And the long
Walk up County O, following
What the old man pointed at

Before he went, those three stars
Coming full circle to bless
The thorn bush I darkened with blood,
And the old Baptist cemetery
Where the Swedes of White Rock lay down
In the winter of '39, my grandfather
Among them, and found home in these stones.

Fishing Off Green's Point at the Start of Spring

Steam rolling all night off
The back channel sloughs,
The cold coming on
And staying past dawn.
I'm here off Green's Point,
Thinking how I belong to none
Of this, not even to the cap
Pulled down over my ears,
Or the old plaid jacket
That someone handed me once
And said was my father's,
And how after a while
It's enough to simply drift here,
With nothing but the wind
Through the stands
Of dead birch, the night
Gone as far as it can go.
And now the last cupful
Of coffee, a bitter sacrament
To the dark and the start
Of spring off Green's Point,
The light coming on
In the empty flyway,
The sound of a freight
Climbing west out of these flood plains.
I think of De Soto,
And how in a few days
This water will cross his bones
A thousand miles from here,
Still hard and gray,

And no more at home than me
As I pull, and watch
The oars crack this cold slate.

Letter Home

Cutting through into the dead trunk,
I thought for a moment
I could cut straight into you,
You and that day you kept this tree up
In the storm, pushing
Until it was the last straight
Thing left on earth,
Until all that the sky gave up
Ran off your cheeks in tears.
Father, that day that began in the dark,
That turned at first light
Into you finding
The limbs and rose bushes
Beaten down, ended with the morning-glories
Opening at noon, ended as blood
On the tall slender trunk
Of the box elder,
As stains on the burlap sack
Of roots. It ended here
With your hands swollen shut,
And me staring at the puffed veins
On your forearms. It ended
As all things did
With no blessings, with your palms
Blossomed with pain, rinsing
In the sink. Dear Father,
Today it ended again
Under a gray sky,
It ended with this saw
Cutting straight through to the heart.

On Tuesdays They Open the Local Pool
To the Stroke-Victims

—for my sons

Thank God my own father didn't have to go through this.
Or I'd be driving him here every Tuesday
So he could swim his laps
Or splash around with the others
In the shallow end. Something terrible
Has been bled out of these lives. Why else
Would they be here pulling themselves along on their sides,
Scissoring, having to prove to their middle-aged sons
They can still dance.
                              The last three days I heard water
In the cellar, the rooms below me bumping together
Like dinghies. Somewhere back in my sleep
My father splashes in the shallow end.
All these men, even
The balding ones waiting behind the chain-link fence
Watching their fathers, are down there
At the bottom of the stairs.
They are all gliding like sunlight,
Like trout across the cold floors of their breeding ponds.

Tornado

Four farms over it looked like a braid of black hemp
I could pull and make the whole sky ring.
And I remember there falling to earth that night
The broken slats of a barn, baling wire, straw and hay,
And one black leather Bible with a broken spine.

I think of the bulls my father slaughtered every August,
How he would pull out of that rank sea
A pair of collapsed lungs, stomach,
Eight bushels of gleaming rope he called intestines,
And one bucket of parts he could never name.

In the dream that keeps coming back in the shape
Of a barn, my father has just drained
His last bull. Outside it is raining harder
Than I've ever seen, and the sky is about to step down
On one leg. And all through the barn,
As high as the loft, the smell of blood and hay.
All night, as long as the dream holds,
He keeps turning the thick slab of soap over and over,
Building the lather up like clouds in his hands.